# 30 Days

## Without

# Social Media

*A Mindfulness Program with a Touch of Humor*

Harper Daniels

**Share your journey!**

**Let people know you're practicing mindfulness! Post a picture of the cover and include #30DaysOff and #30DaysNow via social media. Our various guides share the same lessons, so you can see how others are using mindfulness on their journey!**

This book is meant to be a guide only, and does not guarantee specific results. If the lessons and exercises in this book are followed, change can occur for certain people. Results vary from person to person; some people may not need to complete the thirty days to experience change, but it's encouraged that the entire program be read completely through at least once.

The last half of the book consists of blank note pages that the reader can use in conjunction with the exercises for each day. The reader is encouraged to utilize the note pages; though it's not necessary.

**Give the gift of mindfulness**. See similar guides at www.30DaysNow.com if you wish to purchase a book for a loved one. **See the disclosure below.**

**Disclosure (Shared Lessons and Exercises):**
Keep in mind that our mindfulness guides share the same lessons and exercises, so there is no need to purchase more than one book; unless you are sharing with a group or giving the guides as gifts. Our mindfulness guides are created for various topics; however, they utilize the same lessons and exercises, so please be aware of this before purchasing. For example, *30 Days Without Social Media* will mostly have the same lessons and exercises as *30 Days to Reduce Anxiety* and so forth. By reading just one of our guides, you'll be able to apply the same lessons and exercises to multiple areas of your life.

Enjoy your journey of self-discovery!

# Contents

# Preface

The following pages involve a mindfulness program made up of lessons and exercises to help you through 30 days without social media. Though these lessons and exercises can be applied to any unhealthy reliance, this mindfulness program will focus specifically on the problem of social media dependency.

For some readers, they'll overcome the reliance quickly and will drop their unhealthy attachment in no time; and for others, they'll overcome slowly and gradually. In either case, if you stick with the program you'll start to witness your social media dependency break. Please don't judge your progress in the program, as this isn't a competition and there isn't a goal you must attain. Let the adverse thoughts, feelings, behaviors, and habit simply drop as you work through the exercises and lessons.

It's not necessary to complete the program's days in order, nor should you be religious about completing them successfully. There is no such thing as a successful completion of this program. The bottom line is to observe and awaken, and that cannot be obtained through success, force, pressure, struggle, or competition. Simply relax, follow the program, and the grip of social media will loosen.

You'll also notice that mindfulness, silence, and stillness are a regular discipline for each day in the program. Because you've been influenced by a dependency based society that demands instant gratification, silence and stillness may seem nearly impossible for you to practice. For this reason, we'll incorporate this discipline from the outset. A quiet and still mind is an incredibly powerful resource, but one that requires daily maintenance.

The point of this program is to abstain from social media for 30 days, while substituting mindfulness exercises in its place. It's advised that you post a message to your social media accounts indicating that you're taking a 30 day break – this lets people know why you won't be responding to messages or updating information, and it serves as a natural accountability measure for yourself.

One of the most important lessons to keep in mind is to not fight any anxious or pernicious feelings while participating in this program. Dependencies, habits, and strong patterns of thinking are empowered by a fight and struggle. Social media dependency, like most habits of an imperfect society, feed on negative thought patterns, fear, and struggle. This program will help you overcome the habit without conflict.

You'll need about 15-30 minutes per day for the program; but feel free to spend more time if needed. The amount of time doesn't matter, as long as you're in an environment that allows you to concentrate without distraction.

Also to be mentioned, the last portion of this book includes note pages that you can use with the exercises. It's encouraged that you write down any thoughts, insights, adaptations, lessons, mantras, etc, on those pages. The note pages can also be used to rip out and take with you. Feel free to use them as you wish.

One last thing: If you're like most people, you might be dependent on caffeine, alcohol, or sugar to some extent. If you are, do your best to lessen the consumption of these substances over the next 30 days. It's not necessary that you abstain, but can you cut consumption of these substances in half, or more? It's important that your mind is sober and your body relaxed to make the most of these exercises and lessons.

The next 30 days may be difficult, but they can bring you into a state of awakening. When you're ready: post a message to your social media accounts saying that you won't be available for 30 days, remove all social media apps from your phone, and resolve not to use social media for the next 30 days. If at any time during this program you are tempted to use social media, simply return to this book to continue, or repeat, the exercises, lessons, and mantras.

Let's get started.

*Let others know you're practicing mindfulness! Post a picture of the cover to your social media accounts before starting and include #30DaysOff and #30DaysNow.*

*Share your journey and discover other people practicing mindfulness!*

# Day 1

Exercise:

*Find a place without distraction, and turn off all electronics. Sit with your back straight, kneel, or lie on a hard surface (not bed) and remain in silence for 10 minutes.*

*During these 10 minutes, take deep and focused breaths and hold them for a few seconds each. Exhale slowly. Listen intently to your breathing. Don't try to change it – simply listen, and feel the air go in and out.*

*When you're ready, repeat the mantra: "**Be still. Be silent.**" Repeat this slowly multiple times out loud as well as quietly. You might experience boredom or anxiety, but continue repeating the mantra regardless. Repeat it until you're calm and focused. You can continue the deep breathing during the mantra, or take deep breaths during pauses. Don't rush.*

Each of the 30 days will have this time of silence, focused breathing, and a mantra. Except for this page, the end of each day will remind you of the minutes you are to spend in silence and focused breathing; and will also have a mantra for you to practice. You can repeat the mantras during your times of silence and focused breathing, or following. Remember, there is no right or wrong way to do this.

Dependencies want to fight; in fact, they're energized by fighting. Instead of fighting and struggling with your attachment to social media, meet it with silence and observation. Let the exercises and lessons in this program guide you.

# Day 2

Exercise:

*Ponder this question: Can you remember a time in your life when you weren't using social media?*

Writing is extremely beneficial to the mind; especially when pondering. Write down your thoughts about this particular question. If your mind drifts, then write whatever thoughts emerge. It's okay if you have nothing to write, but ponder the question regardless.

Were you able to remember a period in your life when you weren't using social media on a regular basis? If you're like many people in this modern world, you may have to return to distant memories. It's not uncommon for a person to start using social media at an early age. Entire generations are developing lives online, through social media. The lines of identity are becoming increasingly blurred between online and offline. Like many people today, you've been conditioned to develop an online *you*, while ignoring your offline presence.

Recognize that social media reliance is a learned condition with roots. However, this virtual attachment can be dropped quickly and completely; and you have the capability to drop the reliance. It's time to return to your true being, offline.

*10 minutes of silence and focused breathing. Repeat the mantra: "**Drop. Unlearn. Discover.**"

# Day 3

Exercise:

*On a sheet of paper (any size) write down all the internal lies that you regularly hear about yourself – i.e. within your mind.*

*Now, tear the paper into multiple pieces, and throw away.*

It's common to have an internal voice (or voices) within your mind, playing a record of lies over and over. We eventually begin to accept these lies and let them impact our growth and happiness. Most people you see on a daily basis have these recurring internal voices; and most people are oblivious to them – sort of like white noise. This isn't a mental illness, but a way in which the mind works. We all experience these internal quiet voices whispering untruths about our being. These lies are nothing to fear, but they need to be observed. Writing them down can help you observe and become aware of their deceptions.

The power of silence, focused breathing, and mantras, which you have been practicing, is to draw out the lies. Let them manifest, and observe them. Common internal lies include: *"You are a loser," "You have become nothing, and you will never improve," "You are worthless. No one likes you," "You'll always be alone," "You're a burden,"* and so on. These thoughts are not part of you; however, the deception is to make you believe they are. Like many things in our culture, social media can promise to silence these lies; however, the attachment only feeds them.

*10 minutes of silence and focused breathing. Repeat the mantra: **"Thoughts are only thoughts - nothing more."**

# Day 4

Exercise:

*Say the words "Guilt", "Shame", and "Regret" 10 times to yourself out loud. Don't rush. Pause between each repetition. For the pause, you can take a deep breath. Your eyes can remain open or closed. Again, don't rush - say the words slowly and observe any thoughts, feelings, or images that emerge internally.*

*Now, say these words again 10 times, but with a smile.*

What futile credence we give words such as Guilt, Shame and Regret. We use these words on ourselves as well as others; they become regular vocabulary for our internal recurring voices. And in the end, they're mere words that hold no power. What would these words be without a facial expression, tone, inflection, or emphasis?

When you said these three specific words, what thoughts came to mind, what did you feel, and was there a reaction in your body? If there is a reaction, such as shortness of breath or a frown, people tend to interpret it as sadness; but this reaction is a learned behavior. We've been taught to feel and think a certain way with regard to guilt, shame, and regret. The truth is: these words mean nothing.

Social media addiction, like most dependencies, flourishes on these three words and the learned reactions they produce. But see them for what they are…mere words.

\*10 minutes of silence and focused breathing. Repeat the mantra: **"*I am not Guilt, Shame, or Regret.*"**

# Day 5

Exercise:

*What will your next thought be?*

*Try to guess what your next thought, or next two thoughts, will be.*

Five minutes from now; will you be thinking about love, work, family, a burrito, tomorrow, money, etc? We're not in control of our thoughts, and that scares people. We may be able to influence our thought patterns, but thoughts are more or less like clouds that come and go in a big blue sky. It's difficult to predict what clouds will be floating through our minds this week, let alone in five minutes.

By asking the question, *"What will my next thought be?"* you're allowing yourself to escape a thought cluttered mind for a few moments and experience thoughtlessness – which is fresh, wonderful, new, and present.

After you've attempted to answer that question, observe what thoughts actually do float into your mind. Observe them like you would clouds in the sky. You'll realize that you're not your thoughts, which are often fantasy and not based in the present moment.

The goal of social media is to send you an endless amount of fictitious thoughts; so many that you actually believe they're part of your being. Thoughts are not real.

*10 minutes of silence and focused breathing. Repeat the mantra: **"I am not the thoughts I experience. They will pass."**

# Day 6

Exercise:

*On a piece of paper (any size) write down the name of your current emotion. For example, at this moment you might be feeling agitated, calm, bored, angry, anxious, excited, etc. Whatever emotion you are experiencing, give it a name and put it on paper.*

*Now, write down "I'm experiencing this emotion in the present moment and it will pass. It's only an emotion."*

*You can throw the paper away, or hold onto it if you wish.*

Similar to how we give certain words credence, we tend to give our emotions a lot of trust. We also tend to blame the outside world for emotions we are feeling: *"They made me angry," "I'm depressed because they didn't want me," "If they gave me the job, I would be happy,"* and so on.

The emotions you feel are in you, not in the outer world. No one can cause you to feel or emote in a particular way; if they're able to, it's only because you let them. A great way to let a harmful emotion pass is to observe it; and a good start is by giving it a name and seeing it as powerless.

It's commonplace to blame others for our pain. Instead of seeing the emotion for what it is and letting it pass, we've been taught to rely on dependencies, like social media, to manage the emotional reaction. Wake up! Emotions are not *you*.

*10 minutes of silence and focused breathing. Repeat the mantra: *"I am not an emotion. All emotions will pass."*

# Day 7

Exercise:

*For 5 minutes, hum to yourself with mouth and eyes closed. Take deep breaths between pauses. You can do this exercise lying on a hard floor, standing, kneeling, or sitting with back straight.*

This exercise may seem cliché, but there is a lot that can be learned from the sound of your own voice during a long hum. Humming relaxes the body and mind – similar to listening to rain drops, crickets in the evening, leaves rustling, or a waterfall. It is believed the reason for this relaxing effect involves the wavelengths produced and sent in perpetual flow.

But what's especially interesting about your humming is that it's directly related to your breathing. If you take shorter, rushed breaths, your hum won't be as long and effective; but if you take concentrated, deep breaths, then your hum will serve to relax your body, and possibly bring you into present moment awareness. Also, did you notice that it was you who was relaxing you? You weren't dependent on any other person, thing, or habit to become calm and still. You're able to relax yourself with ease; you are not reliant on social media to relax.

From time to time, listen to yourself hum; listen to the wavelengths you produce from your own being. This is always available to you in the present moment.

*10 minutes of silence and focused breathing. Repeat the mantra: **"Calmness and stillness are always present."***

# Day 8

Exercise:

*Today, look for the color blue in your surrounding environment. If possible, spend the entire day looking for the color blue in the places you go. Whether you're doing this exercise in a bedroom, office, classroom, outside, or while traveling, look for the color blue in all things that surround you. If you think you'll forget to do this throughout the entire day, spend at least 20 focused minutes practicing this exercise at some point.*

Focused attention is something that must be practiced - it doesn't come easy in our rapid paced society. Instead of encouraging us to focus and observe, the modern world encourages us to rush and get things done.

Searching for a color or shape helps to slow down our accelerated and cyclical thought patterns, and reminds us that there's more to the world than the chaotic thoughts we collectively and daily experience. By searching for the color blue, your mind can escape the fictitious grip of anxiety, lust, desire, depression, worry, fear, or any other potent emotion. When you experience a strong desire to use social media, are you aware of the colors around you? Most likely not.

Often, social media functions to distract your conscience from present reality. Look for the color blue today, and wake up to life in the present moment.

*10 minutes of silence and focused breathing. Repeat the mantra: *"I am focused, here and now."*

# Day 9

Exercise:

*Write a letter or email to yourself. There is something about using pen and paper that is very effective when writing letters, but feel free to write an email if you wish. Don't send the letter or email, just write it and save it for a day – you can toss it out or delete it tomorrow.*

*Write anything that comes to mind: It can be advice you want to give yourself, a story from the past, random thoughts and feelings about your social media habit, frustrations and worries, things you're thankful for, etc. There is no right or wrong – write whatever comes to mind in the moment. Try to write at least two full paragraphs.*

What was the theme and voice of your message? Was it a positive or negative tone? Were you advising yourself? Did you make any judgments about yourself? Did you start demanding that you should or should not do something? Was the letter full of gratitude? Was there anger and despair? Read the letter as if you were reading it from a friend – is it a letter that would upset you, or one that you would welcome with excitement and a smile?

Whatever you wrote is essentially being written on the tablet of your mind. This exercise is useful for getting to know the internal voice that we all have in our minds. It's an internal voice that can change for the better with observation, acceptance, and awareness. Be aware of your internal voice in the present moment.

*10 minutes of silence and focused breathing. Repeat the mantra: "**I am not my internal voice. I am aware.**"

# Day 10

Exercise:

*Go out and buy a small trash can. You should be able to find one cheaply. If you don't have the funds for this exercise, you can use an empty box or container; however, a small trash can works better for its symbolism.*

*Designate this specific trash can your "concerns and worries can" (or use any title you wish) – some people benefit from writing this label directly onto the can.*

*Now, write down (on scraps of paper or whatever paper you wish to use) any concerns, worries, and adverse thoughts that you may be experiencing today, and throw them into the can. Try to practice this every day: quickly write down worries, concerns, and negative thoughts, and then throw them into the can. It may be beneficial to have a supply of scrap paper near the can for easy access.*

This exercise may seem simple, but let's go beyond throwing your written concerns, worries, and thoughts away. Designate a few times during the week for sifting through the can and taking out random worries and concerns from days prior – just reach in and pull some out. Observe them, but don't judge yourself. This is a great exercise to learn your negative thought patterns and the lies that grip your conscience. If you stick with this practice, you may gain a deeper understanding into the thought patterns, worries, and concerns that accompany your social media attachment.

*10 minutes of silence and focused breathing. Repeat the mantra: **"There is nothing to worry about. All is well."**

# Day 11

Exercise:

*Imagine this scenario: It is 3:00 AM. You wake up and realize that your home is on fire. Everyone, except you, is out of the house. You realize that you only have a minute or less to get yourself out before everything is destroyed. You must act immediately.*

*With such a short amount of time, what do you grab to take with you?*

Really consider this scenario; because it happens to people every day around the world. People are forced to leave their homes because of fire, flood, violence, and other uncontrollable factors. If this happened to you, what physical things would you grab and take in such a short window of time? Your cell phone, family pictures, computer, passport, specific files, a project, videogame system, or nothing at all? Whatever you take within that moment will be the most meaningful objects to you. What does this tell you about your desires, attachments, concerns, needs, and habits?

Social media attachment supports the illusion that you need an accumulation of online friends, likes, followers, replies, pictures, groups, connections…to feel accepted, belonged, fulfilled, popular, accomplished, satisfied, etc. This is a lie. Think about what is most important to you in the present moment, offline. If your house is burning, hopefully you're not thinking about your social media profile.

\*10 minutes of silence and focused breathing. Repeat the mantra: *"**I am not my online or offline possessions.**"*

# Day 12

Exercise:

*This exercise may seem frivolous, but give it a try; because it may be one of the lessons that benefit you most.*

*For the remainder of the day, whenever you use the bathroom, for any reason, take your time with what you're doing. Don't rush through the process, like you may normally do. Focus on taking your time in the bathroom; do every step of your bathroom experience twice as slow. It may even help to say each step: "I am now sitting up straight on the toilet," "I am now putting soap on my hands," "I am now drying my hands," etc.*

Most people hurry up their bathroom experience, not realizing what they're doing – forcing, not standing or sitting straight, not relaxing, not washing their hands properly, not drying their hands slowly. They rush in and out, like they have somewhere important to go. Don't be like that any longer. Take your time in the bathroom; it's not only unhealthy for the body to rush the excretion process, but it's also unhealthy for the mind.

A rushed bathroom experience doesn't allow you to live in the present moment. Allow the excretion and cleaning to happen naturally with relaxed and focused attention. Similarly, next time you use social media, slow down and think about each step you're taking in the process. Really come into the present moment when checking your social media accounts. Practicing this bathroom exercise will help you slow down.

*10 minutes of silence and focused breathing. Repeat the mantra: **"Don't hurry. Stay present. Stay still."***

# Day 13

Exercise:

*Find a coin. While standing, flip the coin and let it land wherever. If it lands with the head side up, spin around to the right until you come back to your original place; if it lands tail side up, spin around to the left until you come back to your original place. Again, head side up, spin to the right; tail side up, spin to the left – doing a full circle until you return to your original standing position.*

In which direction did you spin? In this exercise you left the direction of your movement completely up to the flip, the coin, and gravity. When you spun, you experienced a specific visual perception of the environment that you would not have had from spinning in the opposite direction. But, you returned to the original position regardless, full circle.

The experience would have been different if you spun to the opposite side; and if you repeat this exercise multiple times, your experiences in the same direction will be different as well. The point being: it doesn't matter what direction you go in or what you experience; you'll always return to the present moment; so the time to be awake, aware, and happy is always now.

Social media addiction will never direct you into present moment happiness - whether you spend one hour or a thousand hours being an *online you*.

*10 minutes of silence and focused breathing. Repeat the mantra: "**The direction does not matter. I am always here and now, in the present moment.**"

# Day 14

Exercise:

*Using objects that can stack (rocks, books, boxes, containers, pillows, etc), stack them slowly and carefully until they fall.*

*When the stack collapses, smile and laugh.*

The lives of many people are spent stacking things for the goal of success, as defined by society. People stack possessions, knowledge, relationships, degrees, money, jobs, toys, businesses, experiences, etc. They stress, fight, fatigue, compete, become ill, and get anxious and depressed through the process of stacking; yet, few people have found happiness. Society tells us that if our stack is high and mighty, we'll have obtained success. What a deception. What are you stacking; or what do you feel compelled to stack? How is your social media attachment supporting that stack?

Allow the stack to fall. This lesson is not encouraging complacency; but instead teaches that real, authentic, and fulfilling relationships and work can only happen apart from the stress and worry of stacking. When you stack, you're focused on the future and the perceived importance of the stack; and then you have to maintain that heap of nonsense, which requires a lot of anxiety and pressure. Focus on your experience in the present moment; and if the stack falls, then smile and laugh.

*10 minutes of silence and focused breathing. Repeat the mantra: **"I allow the stack to fall."**

# Day 15

Exercise:

*On a piece of paper (any size) write down the goals that you've been striving to achieve – i.e. the goals that you believe will bring you fulfillment. For example: a new job, a house in a nice neighborhood, traveling the world, a business, a family, new friends, a degree or certification, building a network, reaching a net worth of a million dollars, etc.*

*Now, tear up the paper into multiple pieces and throw away.*

Goals can be very helpful and useful if they're not obsessed over. However, in the modern world people develop a reliance on goals. Think about all the times you've said something like, *"I need to get that," "I must reach this," "I'll do anything to accomplish that"*, etc. It's often the case that people spend more time worrying about their goals, than freely doing something in the present moment to reach them. Plus, the goal in itself is fleeting, while the journey in the present moment is real and lasting.

The habit of thinking that goals must be met, or else failure ensues, is subtly fixed to dependencies. When you've used social media in the past, what was the goal? What was it that you felt you needed to achieve, obtain, or have?

*10 minutes of silence and focused breathing. Repeat the mantra: **"My happiness does not depend on meeting a goal. I'm happy now."**

# Day 16

Exercise:

*On a piece of paper, write down all the labels and adjectives that you and others use to identify you.*

For example, do you see yourself as a son, daughter, mother, father, student, teacher, cashier, friend, engineer, accountant, employee, employer, roommate, husband, wife, etc? And what adjectives do you use to label yourself; for example, do you identify yourself as failed, successful, happy, depressed, good, moral, unethical, lustful, greedy, valuable, worthless, etc? Don't only write down the labels and descriptions you perceive; but also write down what you believe others label you as: do you believe others see you as a valuable friend, stupid and incompetent employee, extremely smart and talented worker, etc? Take as long as you need, and fill up a sheet of paper with those labels and descriptions.

After you've done that, tear the paper into multiple pieces and throw it away. Those labels and adjectives mean nothing. They're not *you*. You cannot be defined, labeled, described, or controlled by titles. Most people poison their conscience with such learned vocabulary. They really believe these words hold power – they'll even fight, stress out, become ill, and die to make these words part of reality. Social media, as well as most social engines, teaches you to identify with particular words, which are only thoughts. Unlearn them. You are not a label, title, or description.

*15 minutes of silence and focused breathing. Repeat the mantra: "*I am not a label, title, or description.*"

# Day 17

Exercise:

*Lay down on the floor (not on a bed or couch), with your back straight and your arms at your side. Close your eyes.*

*Now, imagine yourself in a coffin or under the ground. If this depresses you, do it regardless. With your eyes closed, imagine not being able to open them ever again; also imagine not being able to move your body or speaking ever again. Stay in this position for 10 minutes, or as long as you can.*

If this seems gothic or dark, that's only your learned perception of the death experience. There's an ancient teaching that says the way to enlightenment is through a keen awareness of death. The person who is daily reminded that the body will die, and faces this fact head on with a clear mind and acceptance, has nothing to lose and is truly free to live in the present moment. The question isn't whether or not your body will die (because it surely will); the more important question is will you live before death?

Will you truly live before your body dies? The present moment is the only thing you'll always experience. Instead of fearing a pending death, accept it and be thankful for the present moment, and live in it! No amount of social media can improve your being in the present; so, while you have the present moment, don't use it by spending too much time on social media.

*15 minutes of silence and focused breathing. Repeat the mantra: **"My body will age and pass, but I will always be present."**

# Day 18

Exercise:

*On a sheet of paper (one that you can easily save and return to later) make a list of hobbies that you've had in the past but have neglected, and also make a list of hobbies that you would like to start in the future.*

*From these lists choose one hobby from the past and one new hobby that you'd like to start. Focus only on these two – the old hobby and the new one. Make this a priority.*

How often have you said, or have heard other people say, *"I wish I had the time."* You do have the time. You just choose to think of time in the way that you've been taught to perceive it. If your life depended on it, you would certainly make the time if needed.

In fact, time is a manmade construct - don't ever forget that. There is only the present moment. Past and future are not here and now. We spend far too much time thinking about time. How many of your recurrent inner thoughts involve questions such as, *"When will that ever happen?"* *"When will I ever change?"* *"Why did that have to happen?"* *"If the past were different, life would be better."* These are lies that only eat into the present moment, and infect our modern world.

Social media addiction occupies the present moment; and that moment could be used to pursue hobbies that magnify your happiness.

*15 minutes of silence and focused breathing. Repeat the mantra: **"The time is now. Happiness is present."**

# Day 19

Exercise:

*Count to 25 slowly, pausing for a few seconds before the next number; then, count backward from 25 slowly. Try this with your eyes closed. While counting up you can imagine yourself being lifted into the sky; and then while counting down, descending back to earth.*

Our world today is about speed. Everyone seems to be in a rush, yet most people are unsatisfied; and, they have no clue where they're going. Chasing the next best thing is a fruitless endeavor. It's the rare person who slows down to enjoy the present moment, regardless of its nature. Because there seems to be so many problems, and most jobs are focused on resolving those problems, people are compelled to accept anxiety and rush toward a reward and conclusion. That surely isn't happiness. Happiness can only be found in the present moment, not in a hypothetical future of rewards and successes. Rushing is another form of going nowhere.

How often have you rushed through your time on social media: scrolling through profiles, perusing pictures, reading comments, checking status updates, watching videos, etc? This is destructive to your peace of mind and health: concentration suffers, stress levels rise, and awareness to the present moment isn't possible.

It's critical to slow down. You only have one life to live – don't rush through it, and don't be dependent on anything that encourages you to rush. Be still, and slow down.

*15 minutes of silence and focused breathing. Repeat the mantra: **"Slow down. Do not rush. Enjoy the present moment."***

# Day 20

Exercise:

*Find a hard object that you can hold in the palm of your hand (such as a stone, ball, or bottle). With either hand, grip this object tightly and squeeze it as hard as you can. Squeeze it forcefully until you can't hold on to it any longer. Drop the object when ready.*

If you could continue squeezing that object forever, perhaps you would; but your muscles and nerves can only endure for so long. At some point, you simply and quickly release the grip and drop the object. There isn't a process to the drop; it just happens when your body says that's enough. The release happens naturally without effort.

Letting go of an unhealthy dependency, habit, thought pattern, addiction, emotion, or behavior can be that easy. Letting go can be as natural and guilt free as dropping the object you were gripping on to so tightly in this exercise; so, take a lesson from your body's experience. When it's time to let go, then let go. The time to let go is always now. Just let the drop happen.

Remember, you don't need social media. By following this program, you've awakened to realize that it's time to drop the attachment and start living in the present moment, offline. So, let the dependency drop.

*15 minutes of silence and focused breathing. Repeat the mantra: **"Letting go is natural. I can let go, here and now."**

# Day 21

Exercise:

*Look at a picture or painting for 10 minutes, alone, in silence, and without any distraction. It would be best if the picture isn't of family or friends, but it could have been created by someone you know. Try to choose a work of art for this exercise, but any physical picture or painting will suffice.*

When social media occupies the mind and present moment, there's a loss of connection to offline images that can be helpful to the awakened mind. The purpose of this exercise is to return the mind to an appreciation of truly inventive and innovative art. A printed picture hanging in a cheap motel room has more artistry than most of the things people look at on social media.

Observing a physical picture, photo, print, or sculpture for an extended period of time can aid the mind in slowing down. You may have had a photo of a landscape hanging in your home for many years, but have you ever taken the time to carefully analyze it? Take some time and do that. Appreciate the image, and observe your thoughts in the process. Don't let images on social media distract you from the beauty that already surrounds you...offline.

*15 minutes of silence and focused breathing. Repeat the mantra: "**Stillness. Silence. Peace. Presence.**"

# Day 22

Exercise:

*Listen to a person intently without interruption. Only speak if the person asks you a question, but don't give a long answer. Make the conversation entirely theirs. Give them the floor, and listen to every word they are saying. Again, do not interrupt. Observe their words and facial expressions without judgment. Be patient and relaxed, even if they speak for more than a few minutes.*

Patience is a dying practice in our digital age. It appears that all business involves the perceived need to go faster, faster, and faster. Quicker responses, faster uploads, more data, rapid analysis, accelerated transportation, and all sorts of chop-chop. This false need for speed has seeped deep into our collective psyche. The modern world is filled with anxiously demanding people, going nowhere fast.

This widespread lack of patience has caused a problem with regard to listening to one another. It has also caused social media dependency to manifest extensively. People addicted to social media are typically in hyper drive; and the social media companies know this. With social media users speeding up their usage, the companies make more revenue. Social media does not encourage patience.

Practicing patience by listening intently to someone speak is a great way to slow down the mind and build meaningful relationships offline. Fabricated relationships with virtual friends cannot compete with real human interaction.

*15 minutes of silence and focused breathing. Repeat the mantra: *"**Listen. Be patient. Listen.**"

# Day 23

Exercise:

*Taste something by eating it very slowly for at least 5 minutes. Pick something with a lot of flavor: a piece of fruit, a strong tea, a spice, soup with many ingredients, honey, etc. Close your eyes through most of your tasting. Savor the piece of food slowly. Pay close attention to the feel of the taste on your tongue. Chew slowly.*

Social media does a great job at stealing presence away from our natural senses, as do many dependencies. Since social media is directly related to our instant pleasure and reward faculties, the more those senses are abused, the more our other senses are neglected, such as taste. When was the last time you thoroughly enjoyed the taste of an orange, vanilla, dark chocolate, olive oil, or cheese? I don't mean enjoying the flavor for a few seconds and then continuing on to eat, but to let the flavor linger before taking another bite.

The taste of a pineapple, pepper, grape, or apple is far more real and satisfying than using social media. It may sound silly to say that, but it's true, because those foods are based in reality. You can actually interact with flavors of various foods in the present, and they don't hypnotize you into an illusory relationship, like that of social media.

Let the taste of food bring you into the present moment.

*15 minutes of silence and focused breathing. Repeat the mantra: "**I am free to taste.**"

# Day 24

Exercise:

*Think of a major worry that consistently upsets you. On a sheet of paper, write down three worst case scenarios for that dominating concern. For example, if someone is persistently worried about going broke, that individual can write as a worst case scenario, "I will end up living on the streets, alone and hungry." As mentioned, write down three worst case scenarios for the worry. The worry doesn't have to be as extreme as going broke; use whichever worry hinders you.*

*Now, next to each of those three worst case scenarios write, "I accept this." You can either toss the paper or keep it.*

Worry is an illness that goes untreated in most people. Think of worry like a cancer of the spirit; but few people know how to treat it effectively. One of the only ways to eradicate worry isn't to fight, ignore, or run from it; but to face it in the present moment and accept it for the illusion it is. You can never be worried about something happening in the present moment – that's impossible; you can only be worried about the future, which is always illusory.

Writing down your worries and worst case scenarios, if they ever do come true (which they rarely do), is a great way to draw those thoughts out of your mind and into the present moment, allowing you to face, accept, and observe them.

*15 minutes of silence and focused breathing. Repeat the mantra: **"Worries are not real. They are passing thoughts."***

# Day 25

Exercise:

*Hold a smile for 5 minutes. You don't need to do this exercise in front of a mirror; but feel free to do so if you wish. You can even do this exercise during the 15 minutes of silence and focused breathing. While holding your smile, take a moment and feel your face; actually touch the smile and the curvature of your lips and cheek bones.*

Have you ever behaved a certain way and then saw your mood change immediately? Physical exercise, such as running and weightlifting, does this for many people. Certain forms of yoga have also been used by people to change their moods. The point is: changing your behavior not only impacts other people, but can also impact your perception of yourself.

You'll notice that while you're smiling during this exercise, you may experience certain emotions. You might feel silly, embarrassed, stupid, funny, weird, or whatever. Continue smiling regardless. In fact, if you are still experiencing temptation to use social media at this point in the program, smile while you're experiencing the feelings – hold the smile until the feelings pass; set a reminder alarm if needed. As always, observe your thoughts while you're smiling; observe the thoughts as if they're clouds passing by in a bright blue sky.

Smiling causes an authentic reaction in our bodies and minds that is essentially good. The present moment enjoys a nice smile. So hold that smile until you no longer can.

*15 minutes of silence and focused breathing. Repeat the mantra: "**Happiness is now. I am happy.**"

# Day 26

Exercise:

*Go for a mindfulness walk for at least 10 minutes. Focus on each step. Feel the steps: the feel of your feet hitting the ground, your heel rolling forward, your toes, the bend of your knees, your hips working to balance your posture, the swinging of your arms, etc. Don't rush; go slow. Focus on your breathing as well. Get in tune with your body. Pay attention to your physical senses throughout the walk. Focus – don't listen to music or be distracted.*

Human beings have always used walking as a naturally restorative exercise. There is something about walking, and focusing on the walk, that calms the mind and soul. The longer one walks, the more relaxed one feels.

Any moment is a good time to walk and experience your inner and outer environment. During long walks, thoughts will emerge that will allow you to consciously observe them. Let the thoughts pass; you may even have emotions that emerge, observe those and let them pass as well. Focusing on your steps will help you clear the mind of clutter. Walking in the early morning and at dusk is especially beneficial.

A 20 minute walk brings more comfort, stillness, peace, focus, and awareness than hundreds of hours of on social media. Walk every day, as much as you can.

*15 minutes of silence and focused breathing. Repeat the mantra: "**I am relaxed. I am at peace.**"*

# Day 27

Exercise:

*Stand in front of a doorway, with the door open. Close your eyes, and take a deep breath. With eyes closed and holding your breath, step through the doorway. Once you have stepped through completely, open your eyes and exhale.*

Doorways are amazing tools that can be used for practicing mindfulness and observation. How often do you rush through doors without paying attention to the change of environment? We don't often pay attention or appreciate the transition; we simply rush through unaware that our perspective has changed. This isn't a bad thing; in fact, it's great that we don't stall in front of doorways, too afraid to enter the next environment. At the beginning of this exercise you were in a particular place, and then you stepped through a doorway into a completely different setting. You made a transition without worry or concern, and very naturally.

When it comes to physical doorways, we rarely stop and worry about the change of environment – we just walk through and accept the new experience. You can apply this same lesson to decisions that have you stressed, anxious, or worried. Step through the decision and accept the change; but try to step through aware and grateful. When you live without the hindrance of social media, and face real life decisions and change head on, there will always be a doorway leading to new experiences.

*15 minutes of silence and focused breathing. Repeat the mantra: **"I accept change with awareness and gratitude."**

# Day 28

Exercise:

*Choose a physical symbol that will remind you to observe and be aware in the present moment. Try to choose something from nature, or that is made of natural material.*

The object you choose can be anything, but it's best if it's something that you can enjoy looking at and touching. For example, many walkers and hikers will find a unique rock small enough to carry in their hands. A stone, necklace, bracelet, seashell, cedar block, coin…anything will do, as long as you enjoy it and you can dedicate it as a tool for remembrance.

Another cunning trick of social media is to confuse the mind into forgetting that you're part of the natural world. Social media requires you to use the imagination, which can be easily manipulated for the business of others. Thus, you're taken out of physical reality. By having a symbol of remembrance, you can reconnect with the present moment. This symbol isn't meant to be an idol, god, or icon. Don't think too deeply into this. The symbol is simply a tool to help you remember where you are in the *here and now*. As long as you're aware of the present, you'll have no desire to return to the hallucination of social media.

*15 minutes of silence and focused breathing. Repeat the mantra: *"**All is well. Here and now, all is well.**"*

# Day 29

Exercise:

*Make yourself laugh for 5 minutes. Don't stop laughing. You might feel strange, weird, embarrassed, or stupid...it doesn't matter, just laugh. Try to laugh alone and without the aid of a comedy or joke. If you don't know how to start, just start making the noises that typically accompany your laughter.*

What feelings did you experience during this exercise? Many people report feeling embarrassed or goofy, which is great; however, most people also report a feeling of relief and buoyancy when they've completed this exercise.

Similar to holding a smile, laughing for 5 minutes is a fantastic way to come into present awareness. If you think about it, humor is necessary for life. How sad is the person who is unable to laugh at the experiences of life? After all, life is funny, even the dreadful and lousy experiences.

If you ever again experience adverse thoughts and feelings that accompany social media attachment, simply laugh at them. Consider how crazy and frivolous social media usage and your reactions to it are; it really is a funny dependency. No other living thing on the planet becomes dependent on virtual platforms and staring at glowing screens. The entire situation is comical. If you perceive the social media attachment for what it truly is - a fictitious, impractical, and frivolous dependency – then it can be easily dropped. You must learn to laugh at it. Genuinely laugh the social media habit away.

*15 minutes of silence and focused breathing. Repeat the mantra: **"Life is wonderful, funny, and real."**

# Day 30

Exercise:

*Take a piece of paper (one that you can keep) and write down all that you are grateful for – these things don't have to be in any particular order of importance.*

*Next to each thing you list, write "Thank you."*

The person who isn't thankful for all that life gives is typically quite miserable; and social media thrives on that misery. The truly grateful person can let go of anything at anytime. A thankful person is always a happy person, so practice gratitude daily.

Have you ever heard anyone say, *"I'm so grateful for my dependence on social media"*? Nobody is thankful for a social media habit; which is a clear and telling sign that it's a destructive dependency. However, a few people have learned to be thankful for the present moment experience.

Not only is it unhealthy, but dependency on social media discourages a grateful mind and soul. With only one life to live in the present moment, it's important to always emphasize a grateful heart. Spend time with people who are grateful, and do things that nourish a thankful heart in the present moment. Anything that encourages misery and depression isn't worth giving attention to. Be thankful, always.

*15 minutes of silence and focused breathing. Repeat the mantra: **"I am grateful. I am thankful."***

# Conclusion

The exercises and lessons in this program taught and encouraged observation, awareness to your present moment experience, change of perception, and awakening to true happiness, which can only be found here and now. You were shown that your negative thoughts and feelings are not caused by social media, or any unhealthy reliance, but are solely within you and illusory; which means that you are capable of letting those thoughts and feelings pass and dropping the social media attachment.

As mentioned at the beginning, there were no goals or measures of success for this program. If you were hoping to find a reason to spend more or less time on social media, then you may be spending too much time struggling and thinking about the habit. This was not meant to be a struggle, but a release from an adverse attachment to social media.

Life is not meant to be spent attached to social media, or any toxic dependency. Wake up to the present moment and enjoy your present experience. If you've made it through the program, you are certainly more awakened than when you started; however, don't give up mindfully practicing observation of thoughts and feelings, stillness, silence, deep and focused breathing, allowing everything to pass, laughing, smiling, and being grateful.

Live wonderfully awakened and aware, and enjoy your present moment offline.

# *Notes for Day 1*

(Use this page to write down thoughts, reminders, ideas, prayers, mantras, revelations, lessons, modifications to the exercise, or experiences.)

# *Notes for Day 2*

(Use this page to write down thoughts, reminders, ideas, prayers, mantras, revelations, lessons, modifications to the exercise, or experiences.)

# *Notes for Day 3*

(Use this page to write down thoughts, reminders, ideas, prayers, mantras, revelations, lessons, modifications to the exercise, or experiences.)

# *Notes for Day 4*

(Use this page to write down thoughts, reminders, ideas, prayers, mantras, revelations, lessons, modifications to the exercise, or experiences.)

# *Notes for Day 5*

# *Notes for Day 6*

(Use this page to write down thoughts, reminders, ideas, prayers, mantras, revelations, lessons, modifications to the exercise, or experiences.)

# Notes for Day 7

(Use this page to write down thoughts, reminders, ideas, prayers, mantras, revelations, lessons, modifications to the exercise, or experiences.)

# *Notes for Day 8*

(Use this page to write down thoughts, reminders, ideas, prayers, mantras, revelations, lessons, modifications to the exercise, or experiences.)

# *Notes for Day 9*

(Use this page to write down thoughts, reminders, ideas, prayers, mantras, revelations, lessons, modifications to the exercise, or experiences.)

# Notes for Day 10
(Use this page to write down thoughts, reminders, ideas, prayers, mantras, revelations,
lessons, modifications to the exercise, or experiences.)

# *Notes for Day 11*

(Use this page to write down thoughts, reminders, ideas, prayers, mantras, revelations, lessons, modifications to the exercise, or experiences.)

# *Notes for Day 12*

(Use this page to write down thoughts, reminders, ideas, prayers, mantras, revelations, lessons, modifications to the exercise, or experiences.)

# *Notes for Day 13*

(Use this page to write down thoughts, reminders, ideas, prayers, mantras, revelations,
lessons, modifications to the exercise, or experiences.)

# *Notes for Day 14*

(Use this page to write down thoughts, reminders, ideas, prayers, mantras, revelations, lessons, modifications to the exercise, or experiences.)

_____

_____

_____

_____

_____

_____

_____

_____

_____

_____

_____

_____

_____

_____

_____

_____

_____

_____

_____

_____

_____

_____

_____

_____

_____

_____

# *Notes for Day 15*

(Use this page to write down thoughts, reminders, ideas, prayers, mantras, revelations, lessons, modifications to the exercise, or experiences.)

# *Notes for Day 16*

(Use this page to write down thoughts, reminders, ideas, prayers, mantras, revelations, lessons, modifications to the exercise, or experiences.)

# Notes for Day 17

(Use this page to write down thoughts, reminders, ideas, prayers, mantras, revelations, lessons, modifications to the exercise, or experiences.)

# *Notes for Day 18*

(Use this page to write down thoughts, reminders, ideas, prayers, mantras, revelations, lessons, modifications to the exercise, or experiences.)

# *Notes for Day 19*

(Use this page to write down thoughts, reminders, ideas, prayers, mantras, revelations, lessons, modifications to the exercise, or experiences.)

# *Notes for Day 20*

# *Notes for Day 21*

(Use this page to write down thoughts, reminders, ideas, prayers, mantras, revelations, lessons, modifications to the exercise, or experiences.)

_____

_____

_____

_____

_____

_____

_____

_____

_____

_____

_____

_____

_____

_____

_____

_____

_____

_____

_____

_____

_____

_____

_____

_____

_____

_____

_____

_____

# *Notes for Day 22*

# Notes for Day 23

(Use this page to write down thoughts, reminders, ideas, prayers, mantras, revelations, lessons, modifications to the exercise, or experiences.)

# Notes for Day 24

(Use this page to write down thoughts, reminders, ideas, prayers, mantras, revelations, lessons, modifications to the exercise, or experiences.)

# *Notes for Day 25*

(Use this page to write down thoughts, reminders, ideas, prayers, mantras, revelations, lessons, modifications to the exercise, or experiences.)

# Notes for Day 26

(Use this page to write down thoughts, reminders, ideas, prayers, mantras, revelations, lessons, modifications to the exercise, or experiences. If you'd like to share online, please post using **#30DaysNow** or use the exercise's unique hashtag.)

# *Notes for Day 27*

(Use this page to write down thoughts, reminders, ideas, prayers, mantras, revelations, lessons, modifications to the exercise, or experiences.)

# *Notes for Day 28*

# *Notes for Day 29*

(Use this page to write down thoughts, reminders, ideas, prayers, mantras, revelations, lessons, modifications to the exercise, or experiences.)

# *Notes for Day 30*

(Use this page to write down thoughts, reminders, ideas, prayers, mantras, revelations, lessons, modifications to the exercise, or experiences.)

To be mindful is to experience life in the present moment...it's the only moment we have.

*Don't forget to leave an online review.*

*Thank you!*

Made in United States
Orlando, FL
11 November 2023

38836550R00061